The
Sacred Colle

High Voice

Compiled and Edited by Richard Walters

ISBN 0-634-03072-8

HAL•LEONARD®
CORPORATION

7777 W. BLUEMOUND RD. P.O. BOX 13819 MILWAUKEE, WI 53213

Visit Hal Leonard Online at
www.halleonard.com

Contents

Concert Arrangements of
Hymns & Sacred Folksongs

arranged by Richard Walters

Contents

Alphabetically by Title

Agnus Dei
(Lamb of God)

Georges Bizet

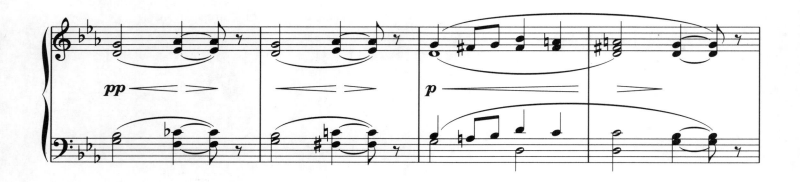

8

Ave Maria

César Franck
(1822 - 1890)

Ave Maria

Franz Schubert

A - - ve Ma - ri - a!
A - - ve Ma - ri - a!

dim.

Ave Maria
(adapted from "Prelude in C" by J.S. Bach)

Charles Gounod

e - ri - bus et _____ be - ne -

dic - tus fruc - tus_____

ven - tris _____ tu - i Je -

sus. _____ Sanc - ta Ma -

Be Near Me Still

Prayer

English version by
Alma Strettell

Ferdinand Hiller, Op. 46

du mei - ne Stär - ke, mein Son - nen - licht,
my pow'r un - shak - en, My soul's true sun,

bis an das En - de mei - ner Ta - ge, sei du mit
Till earth's dark days shall be for - sak - en, Be near me

mir, sei du mit mir, bis an das En - de mei - ner
still! be near me still! Till earth's dark days shall be for -

Ta - ge, sei du mit mir, mit mir.
sak - en, Be near me, near me still!

Clouds and Darkness

Antonín Dvořák, Op. 99

Meno maestoso

trem - bled. Moun - tains shall melt as wax ___ at ___ His ___

pres - ence, when the Might - y One com - eth to judg - ment. The

heav - ens de - clare His truth and right - eous - ness, and all the earth re - joic - eth in His

great - ness.

Sundquist Studio Class Singing Assignments
Everyone must sign up *AT LEAST* 3 times!

February 22:

_____
_____
_____

March 1:

_____
_____
_____

March 8:

_____
_____
_____

March 15:
Spring Break!

March 22:

_____
_____
_____

March 29:

_____
_____
_____

April 5:

_____
_____
_____

April 12:

_____
_____
_____

April 19:

_____

_____

_____

April 26:

_____

_____

_____

Lord, Thou Art My Refuge

Antonín Dvořák

ye that do e - vil, for my heart is fixed, I will hold fast to God's com-mand - ments.

Streng-then me, that I may keep ___ Thy law, and that Thy stat - utes may be my ___ de - light.

Hear My Prayer

Antonín Dvořák

face from my pe - ti - tion.

Bow thine ear to me and

heark - en un - to the voice of my mourn - ing,

to the voice of my mourn - ing.

Pain - ed sore is my

heart with-in, and trem - bling hath fal - len up-

on me, the fear of death o - ver -

dove! Far a - way _____ would I wan - der, I would hide me in the wil - der - ness. On wings I would has - ten to hide from the storm, the storm ___ and fear - ful tem - pest.

God Is My Shepherd

Antonín Dvořák

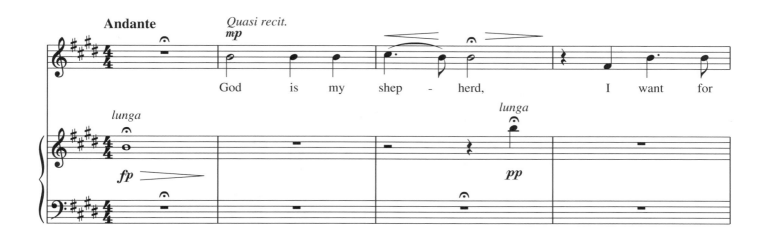

God is my shep - herd, I want for

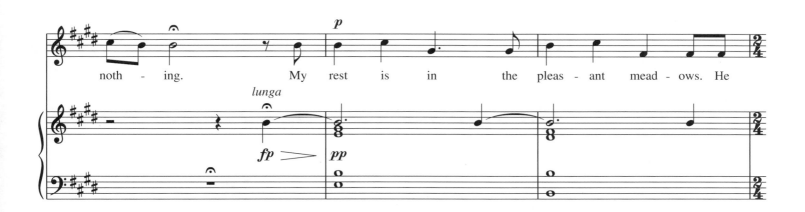

noth - ing. My rest is in the pleas - ant mead - ows. He

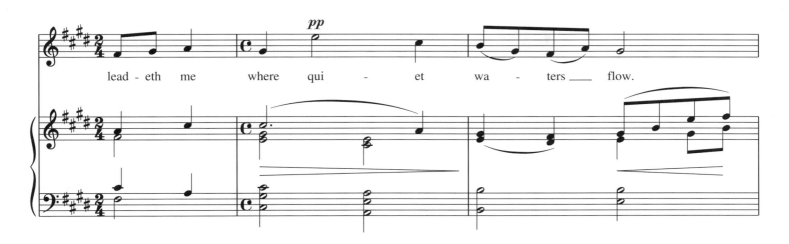

lead - eth me where qui - et wa - ters ___ flow.

My faint - ing soul doth

He re - store and guid - eth me in the ways of peace, to

glo - ri - fy His name. _____ And

though in death's dark val - ley my steps must

wan - der, my spir - it shall __ not fear, for

Thou art by me __ still.

Thy __ rod and staff are with me, and they shall __ com - fort

me.

I Will Sing New Songs

Antonín Dvořák

By the Waters of Babylon

Antonín Dvořák

Hear My Prayer, O Lord

Antonín Dvořák

Thou art in - deed my God, yea, I will seek Thee early. My soul is faint, my bod - y long - eth, long - eth af - ter Thee in a bar - ren de - sert where there is no wa - ter.

Now I will bless Thee dai - ly and lift my hands in pray'r and ad - o - ra - tion; yea, my lips shall praise Thee all my life long.

Turn Thee to Me

Antonín Dvořák

great are the sor-rows of my _ heart; bring me out of my _____ dis-

tress, bring me out of my _____ dis-

tress. Oh be mer-ci-ful,

look on my sor-row, see mine af-flic-tion and for-give me all my

I Will Lift Mine Eyes

Antonín Dvořák

Andante con moto

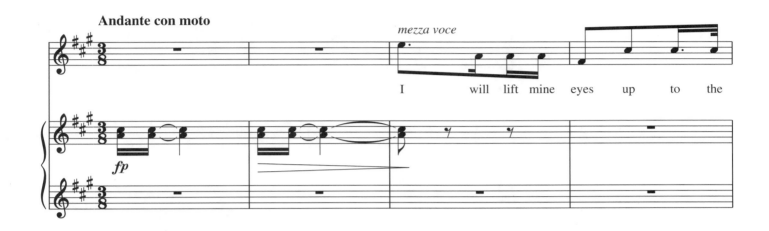

mezza voce

I will lift mine eyes up to the

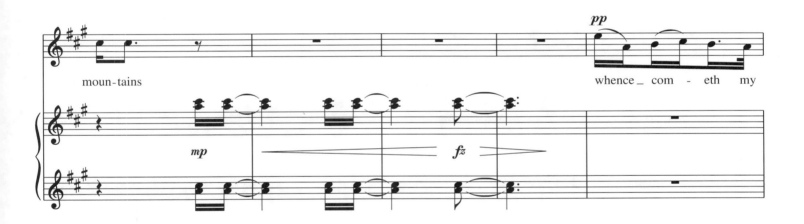

moun-tains

whence _ com - eth my

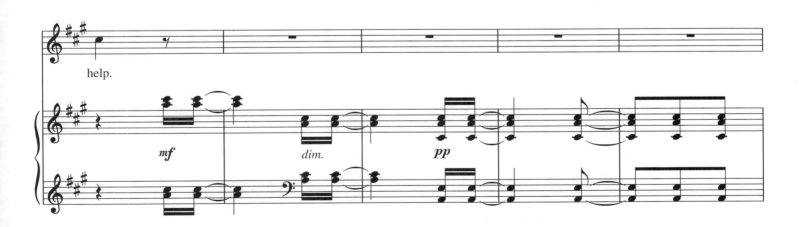

help.

58

keep-eth thee will not slum - ber. Be -

hold, the keep - er of Is - ra - el is

He that slum - bers not _____ nor

sleeps.

Sing Ye a Joyful Song

Antonín Dvořák

Allegro moderato

corn, and let _____ all the trees _____ of the for -

rit.   *a tempo*

- est be joy - ful!

rit.   **ff**   *f*

a tempo

rit.

f

Dank sei Dir, Herr
(Thanks Be to God)

Siegfried Ochs*
(Previously attributed to Handel)

*Siegfried Ochs (1858-1929) claimed to have discovered an aria by Handel, and to have made an arrangement of the piece, which was published and became well-known. Closer research has revealed that this is actually an original composition by Ochs.

66

- ra - el hin durch das Meer.
grate - ful thanks be to Thee.

68

Bist du bei mir

(You Are with Me)

Gottfried Heinrich Stölzel
(Previously attributed to J.S. Bach)

Anonymous

Bist du bei mir, geh' ich mit
You are with me, my joy for -

Freu - den zum Ster - ben und zu mei - ner
ev - er. Un - til my death and un - to my

Ruh', zum Ster - ben und zu mei - ner Ruh'.
rest, un - til my death and un - to rest.

Bist du ____ bei ____ mir, geh' ich mit
You are ____ with ____ me, my joy for-

Freu - den zum Ster - ben ____ und zu mei - ner ____
ev - er. Un - til ____ my ____ death and un - to my

Ruh', zum ____ Ster - ben und zu mei - ner Ruh'.
rest, un - til ____ death and un - to rest.

Ach, wie ver - gnügt wär' so mein
Oh, how con - tent all of my

72

En - de,   Es drück - ten ___ dei - ne schö - nen ___
earth - ly days,   And at ___ the ___ end will your ___ warm and

Hän - de mir ___ die ge - treu - en Au - gen zu.
lov - ing hand reach to ___ gent - ly ___ close my eyes.

Ach, wie ver - gnügt   wär' so mein
Oh how con - tent   all of my

En - de,   Es drück - ten ___ dei - ne schö - nen ___
days ___   And at ___ the ___ end will your ___ warm and

Crucifixus

Jean-Baptiste Faure

Entreat Me Not to Leave Thee

(Song of Ruth)

From the Book of Ruth 1:16-17

Charles Gounod

where thou lodg - est, I will lodge. _____ Thy

un poco meno presto, ma pochissimo

peo - ple shall be my peo - ple,

and thy ___ God, my God; _____ thy

peo - ple shall be my peo - ple, and thy

bur - ied; ___ The Lord do so to me, and more al - so, if aught but

death part thee and me, if aught but death ___ part thee and

me. _____ Thy peo - ple shall be my

p

peo - ple, and thy ___ God, my

84

God,   my   God.

Evening Hymn

Words by Dr. William Fuller
Music by Henry Purcell
Realization by Richard Walters

88

Evening Prayer

from *Hansel and Gretel*

Engelbert Humperdinck

When I rest my wea - ry head an - gels gath - er 'round my ___ bed; ___

Keep - ing me from harm's way, Guid - ing me through

night and day. Some stay by my right side,

Oth - ers by my left side. Ev - er may your watch be. Al - ways you will guide me. An - gels ev - er with your might Please bless and guard my soul _____ to - night.

He That Keepeth Israel

Adolphe Schlösser

slum - bers not, nor sleeps. _____ He will give his

An - gels charge o - ver thee, To keep thee in

all thy ways, _____ in all thy ways, He that

keep - eth Is - ra - el, _____ He that

The Holy City

F. E. Weatherly and Stephen Adams

Last night I lay a-sleep-ing There came a dream so fair. I
then me-thought my dream was changed, the streets no long - er rang.

stood in old Je - ru - sa - lem, Be - side the tem - ple there; I
Hushed were the glad Ho - san - nas The lit - tle child - ren sang; The

heard the child-ren sing-ing, And ev - er as they sang, Me -
sun grew dark with mys - ter - y, The morn was cold and chill As the

Lift up your gates and sing,
Hark how the an - gels sing,
Ho -
san - na in ___ the high - est, Ho -
san - na ___ to your King!
And

affret. poco a poco

And once a-gain the scene was changed, New earth there seemed to __ be, I

saw the Ho - ly Ci - ty Be - side the tide - less sea; The

light of God was on its streets, The gates were o - pen wide, And

cantabile

all who would might en - ter, And

o'er! Ho - san - na in the high - est, Ho -

- san - na__ for - ev - er - more! Ho -

san - na in the high - est,__ Ho - san - na__ for ev - er -

ad lib.

colla voce

more!

Jesu, Joy of Man's Desiring

Johann Sebastian Bach
arranged by John Reed

108

light.
springs.

Word of God, our flesh _____ that fash - ion'd
Theirs is beau - ty's fair - est plea - sure,

With the fire of
Theirs is wis - dom's

110

throne.
known.

O Divine Redeemer
(Repentir)

Charles Gounod

114

116

118

Just a Closer Walk with Thee

Traditional American Song
arranged by Richard Walters

Grant it Je-

sus is my plea,_____

Dai - ly walk - ing close to Thee,_____

let it be,____ dear Lord,_ let it be._

The Palms
(Les Rameaux)

Jean-Baptiste Faure

Andante maestoso

O'er all the way, green palms and
Sur nos che-mins les ra-meaux

blos - soms gay.
et les fleurs.

Are strewn this day in fes - tal
Sont ré - pan-dus dans ce grand

pre - - par - a - tion; Where Je - sus comes to wipe our
jour _____ de fê - te, Jé - sus s'a - van - ce, il vient sé -

tears a - way, E'en now the throng to wel - come
cher a nos pleurs, Dé - jà la fou - le à l'ac - cla -

Him pre - pare; Join all and sing, _____ His
mer s'ap - prête; Peu - ples, chan - tez, _____ chan -

name _____ de-clare Let ev - 'ry voice re - sound in
tez _____ en chœur, Que vo - tre voix á no - tre

Bless Him who com-eth to bring us sal - va - tion!

Bé - ni ce - lui qui vient sau - ver le mon - de!

Optional high notes are for the final verse.

Panis Angelicus

César Franck

pau - per, ser - vus et hu - mi - lis,

ff

Pau - per, — pau - per, ser - vus, — ser - vus et

hu - mi - lis.

decresc.

p

There Is a Green Hill Far Away

Charles Gounod

There is a green hill far a-way, With- out a cit-y-wall, Where the dear Lord was cru-ci-fied, Who

Saved by His pre - cious blood. There was no oth - er

good e - nough To pay the price of

sin, He on - ly could un -

lock the gate Of Heav'n and let us in. O

dim. p p

p cresc.

molto espress.

f dim. p

try His works to do!

We must love Him, too!

We must love Him, too, And try His works to

dim. *p*

do!

pp

Balm in Gilead

Jeremiah 8 : 22

African-American Spiritual
arranged by Harry T. Burleigh

heal the sin - sick soul. Some - times I feel dis -
cour - aged, And think my work's in vain, But
then the Ho - ly Spir - it, Re - vives my soul a -
gain ___ There ___ is a Balm in Gil - e - ad, to

By An' By

African-American Spiritual
arranged by Harry T. Burleigh

Deep River

African-American Spiritual
arranged by Harry T. Burleigh

Couldn't Hear Nobody Pray

African-American Spiritual
arranged by Harry T. Burleigh

Didn't My Lord Deliver Daniel

story from
the Book of Daniel
chapter 6

African-American Spiritual
original arrangement by
Harry T. Burleigh
adapted by Richard Walters

Gos - pel ship, and the ship it be - gin __ to __ sail. It land - ed me o - ver on

cresc. *mp*

Ca - naan's shore, __ and I'll nev - er come back __ an - y - more. My Lord de -

f

f

opt.

liv - er Dan - iel, He de - liv - er Dan - iel. He de - liv - er Dan - iel. __ Did - n't

molto rit. *opt.* *a tempo* *opt.*

my Lord de - liv - er Dan - iel, __ and why not ev - er - y man? _____

molto rit. *a tempo* *8va - - - -*

Don't You Weep When I'm Gone

Jeremiah 22:10

African-American Spiritual
arranged by Harry T. Burleigh

moth - er meet me there, moth - er, meet me in the air, O _____ moth - er don't you weep when I am gone. When I'm gone, gone, When I'm gone, gone, gone ___ O _____ moth - er, don't you weep when I am gone.

He's Just the Same Today

Exodus 14 : 22
1 Samuel 17 : 49

African-American Spiritual
arranged by Harry T. Burleigh

front of him ___ the sea; God rais'd the wa - ters

like a ___ wall an' o - pen'd up ___ the way _____ An' the

God that ___ liv'd in Mo - ses ___ time is just ___ the same ___ to -

day. Is ___ jus' the same ___ to - day ___

Jus' _____ the _____ same to-day; An' the God that __ liv'd in

cresc.

rit.   _a tempo_

Mo - ses __ time, is jus' the same __ to - day.

rit.   _a tempo_   _f_

_mf_

When

Da - vid an' __ Go - li - ah met __ the wrong a - gainst __ the

164

Go Down, Moses
(Let My People Go!)

Exodus 8

African-American Spiritual
arranged by Harry T. Burleigh

Helena,

Thank you for your kind help.
Here is Laura's book. She has
looked at "Come. Thou Fount" & "How Firm
a Foundation" (p265) She selected the
second as an encore or a "just in case".
Thank you again. We'll be up here
at 3:00pm.

Rick

for Kimm

Come, Thou Fount
of Every Blessing

Robert Robinson, 1758

American Folk Tune
First set by John Wyeth, 1813
arranged by Richard Walters

Go, Tell It on the Mountain

African-American Spiritual
arranged by Harry T. Burleigh

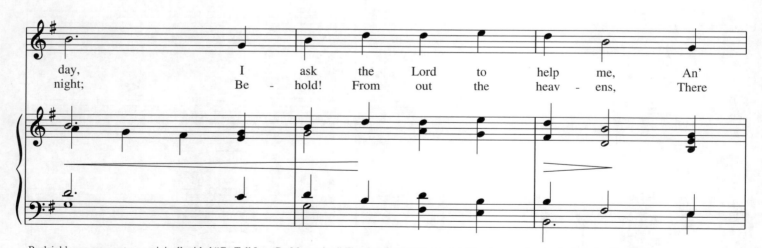

Burleigh's arrangement was originally titled "Go Tell It on De Mountains." The singular form "mountain" has become the standard version for this song.

The Gospel Train

African-American Spiritual
arranged by Harry T. Burleigh

The gos - pel train is a - com - in', I hear it jus' at

han', ___ I hear the car - wheels rum - blin', An' roll - in' thru the

I Don't Feel No-Ways Tired

Hebrews 11:14, 16

African-American Spiritual
arranged by Harry T. Burleigh

glo - ry Hal - le - lu - jah!

There's a bet - ter day _ a - com - in' Hal - le - lu -

jah There's a bet - ter day _ a - com - in' Hal - le - lu. _____ When I

leave this worl' _ of __ sor - row, Hal - le - lu - jah For to

I Stood on the River of Jordan

African-American Spiritual
arranged by Harry T. Burleigh

Andante cantabile

Sis - ter
Broth-er } you bet - ter be read - y, To see that ship sail by.

Oh, mour-ner don't you weep, When you see that ship come sail - in' o - ver,

Shout Glo - ry Hal - le - lu - jah! When you see that ship sail

by. I stood on the riv - er of Jor - dan!

I Want to Be Ready

Revelation 21 : 16
Acts 2

African-American Spiritual
arranged by Harry T. Burleigh

187

Let Us Cheer the Weary Traveler

African-American Spiritual
arranged by Harry T. Burleigh

Little David, Play on Your Harp

African-American Spiritual
arranged by Harry T. Burleigh

Lit - tle Da - vid, play on your harp, Hal - le - lu, _____

decresc.

pp

Lit - tle Da - vid, play on your harp, Hal - le - lu, _____

pp

rit. e dim.

(mezzo voce)
a tempo
p _opt._

Lit - tle Da - vid, play on your harp, Hal - le - lu. _____

rit. e dim.

a tempo
p   **f**

pp

My Lord, What a Mornin'

text based on
the Book of Revelation, 8 : 10

African-American Spiritual
arranged by Harry T. Burleigh

Nobody Knows the Trouble I've Seen

African-American Spiritual
arranged by Harry T. Burleigh

Poco Adagio

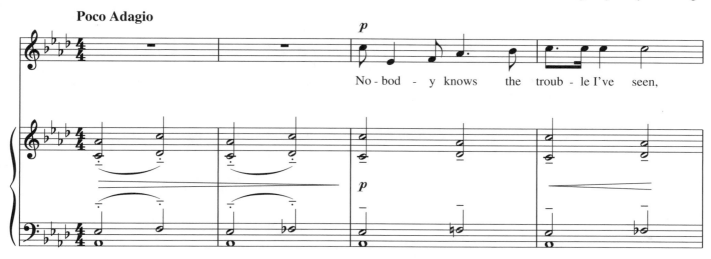

No - bod - y knows the troub - le I've seen,

No - bod - y knows but Je - sus. No - bod - y knows the troub - le I've seen,

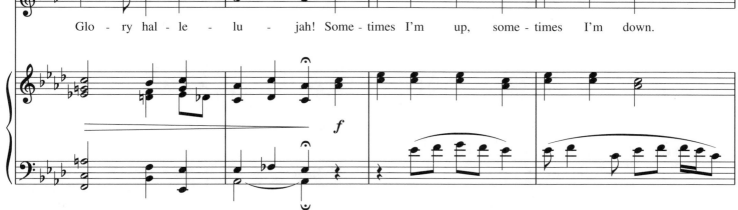

Glo - ry hal - le - lu - jah! Some - times I'm up, some - times I'm down.

My Way's Cloudy

African-American Spiritual
arranged by Harry T. Burleigh

O Rocks, Don't Fall on Me

African-American Spiritual
arranged by Harry T. Burleigh

Oh, Didn't It Rain

Genesis 7 : 4

African-American Spiritual
arranged by Harry T. Burleigh

Moderato

rit. *a tempo*

For-ty days for-ty nights when the rain kept a-fall-in', The

wick-ed climb the tree, an' for help kept a-call-in', For they

heard the wa-ters wail-in' Didn't it rain,

crescendo

heard the wa-ters roar-in' Didn't it rain, __ rain, __ didn't it rain, __

p   *crescendo*   *f*   *ff*

No - ah
Tell me No - ah, __

molto rit. opt.
rit.   *mf molto rit.*

didn't _ it rain __   Didn't it rain.

a tempo   *opt.*   *p*
a tempo

Sinner, Please Don't Let
This Harvest Pass

African-American Spiritual
arranged by Harry T. Burleigh

lose __ your soul at last. _____ I know that __ my Re - deem - er

lives _____ I know that __ my Re - deem - er

lives _____ I know that __ my Re -

deem - er lives Sin - ner please don't let this har - vest

pass _____ My God is a might-y man of war _____

My God is a might-y man of war _____

My God is a might - y man of

war Sin-ner please don't let this har-vest pass _____

Sometimes I Feel
Like a Motherless Child

African-American Spiritual
arranged by Harry T. Burleigh

'Tis Me, O Lord

African-American Spiritual
arranged by Harry T. Burleigh

Steal Away

African-American Spiritual
arranged by Harry T. Burleigh

Adagio e molto espressivo

Steal a-way, steal a-way, steal a-way to Je - sus!

Steal a-way, steal a-way home, I ain' got long to stay here!

My Lord, calls me, He calls me by the thun - der; The

224

Swing Low, Sweet Chariot

African-American Spiritual
arranged by Harry T. Burleigh

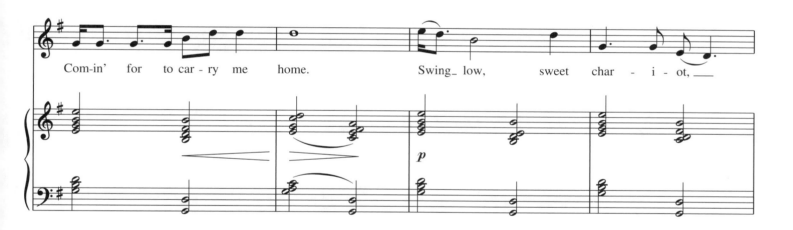

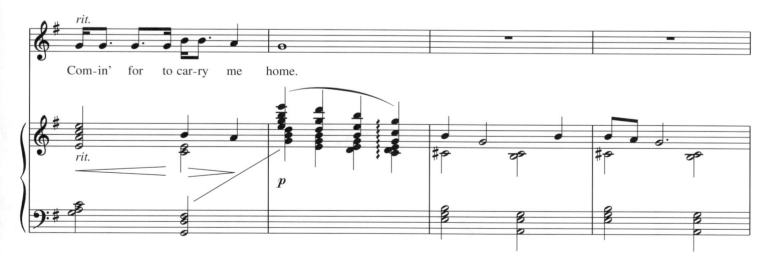

Wade in the Water

African-American Spiritual
arranged by Harry T. Burleigh

Weepin' Mary

John 20 : 11

African-American Spiritual
arranged by Harry T. Burleigh

You May Bury Me in the East

1 Corinthians 15 : 52

African-American Spiritual
arranged by Harry T. Burleigh

poco rit.　　　　a tempo

hear the trum - pet soun'³ _____ in that morn - in'; In that

poco rit.　　　a tempo

rit.

morn - in', my Lord, How I long³ _ to go: For to

rit.
p

a tempo

hear the trum - pet soun' _ in that morn - in'. _____

a tempo
p
decresc.

_____ In that dread - ful judg - ment day, I'll take

sfz

for Steve

Be Thou My Vision

Ancient Irish
translated by Mary E. Byrne, 1905
versified by Eleanor H. Hull, 1912

Traditional Irish Melody
arranged by Richard Walters

Be thou my __ vi - sion, O Lord of my

heart, Naught be all else to me save that thou art.

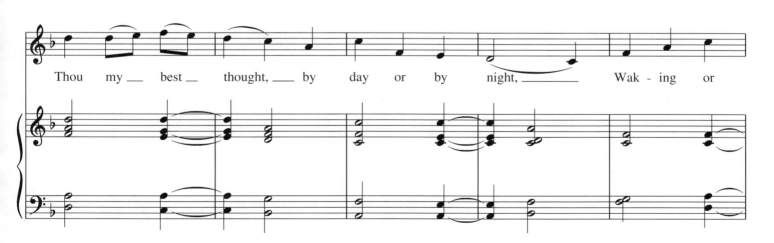

Thou my __ best __ thought, __ by day or by night, __ Wak - ing or

dwell - ing, and __ I with Thee one. ___

8va -

(8) -

Rich - es I __ need not, nor man's emp - ty

p   *mp*

praise. _____   Thou mine in - her - i - tance,

now and al - ways; _____   Thou and __ thou __

240

May I reach heav'n's joys, O bright heav-en's sun!

Heart of ___ my ___ own heart, what - ev - er be - fall, ___

Still be my vi - sion, O ru - ler of all. ___

* From here to the end maybe either *piano* or *forte,* depending on the singer's best attributes.

for Sharon

Ah, Holy Jesus

Johann Heermann, 1630
translated by Robert S. Bridges, 1899

"Herzliebster Jesu"
Johann Crüger, 1640
arranged by Richard Walters

Ah, ho-ly Je-sus, how hast thou of-fend-ed,

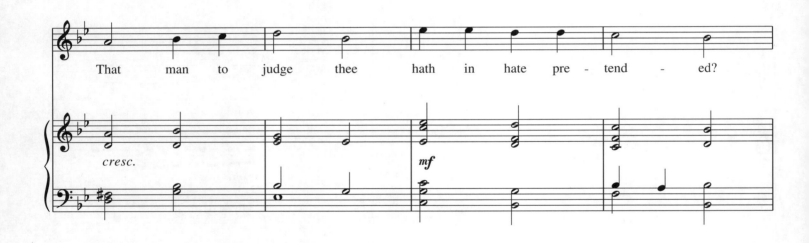

That man to judge thee hath in hate pre-tend-ed?

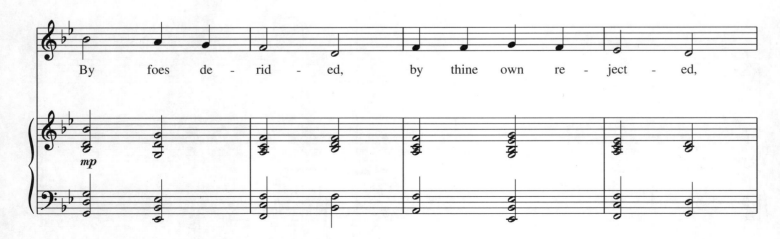

By foes de-rid-ed, by thine own re-ject-ed,

O most af - flict - ed! Who was the

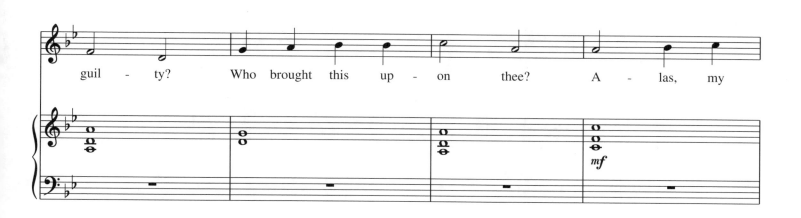

guil - ty? Who brought this up - on thee? A - las, my

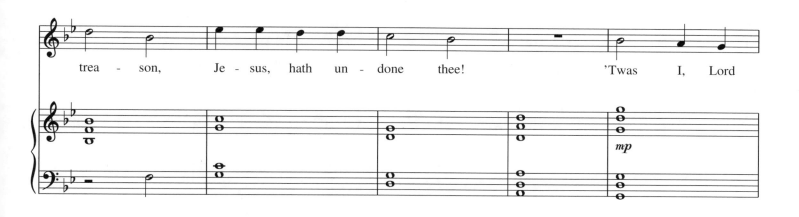

trea - son, Je - sus, hath un - done thee! 'Twas I, Lord

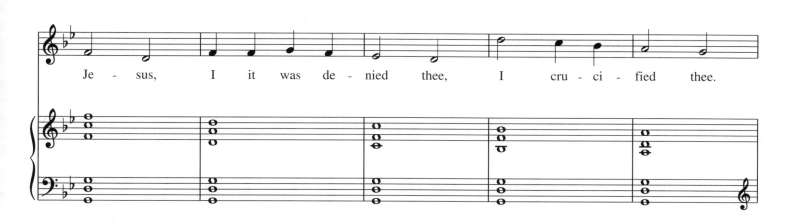

Je - sus, I it was de - nied thee, I cru - ci - fied thee.

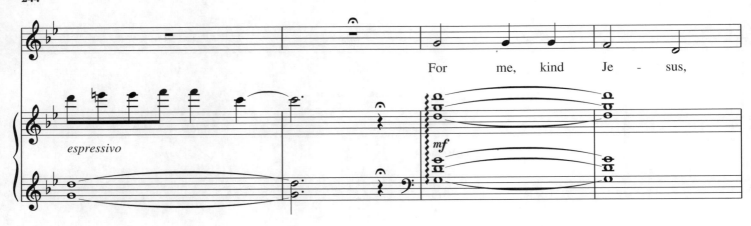

For me, kind Je - sus,

was thy in - car - na - tion, Thy mor - tal sor - row,

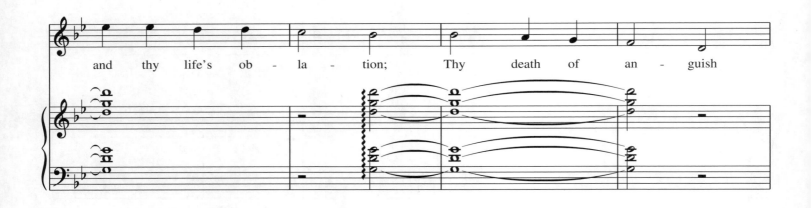

and thy life's ob - la - tion; Thy death of an - guish

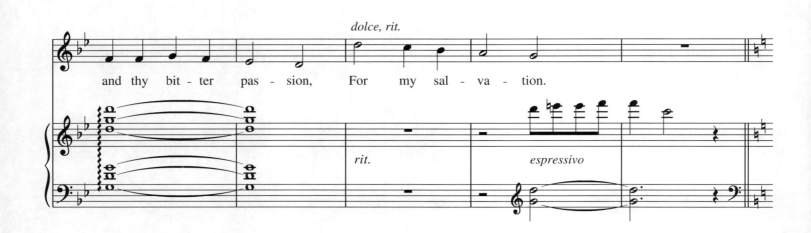

dolce, rit.

and thy bit - ter pas - sion, For my sal - va - tion.

for Carol and Anne

All Creatures of Our God and King

after Psalm 148
Francis of Assisi, c. 1225
translated by William Draper (alt.)

"Lasst uns Erfreuen"
melody from
Geistliche Kirchengesäng, Cologne 1623
adapted by Ralph Vaughan Williams, 1906
arranged by Richard Walters

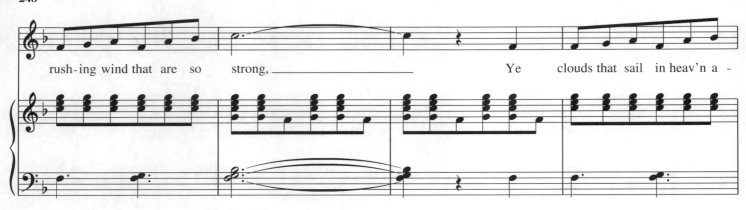

rush-ing wind that are so strong, _____ Ye clouds that sail in heav'n a -

long, _____ O ___ praise Him, Al - le - lu - ia! _____

___ Thou ris - ing morn, in praise re - joice, _____ Ye

lights of eve-ning, find a voice, _____ O ___ praise Him, O ___

praise Him, _____ Al - le - lu - ia, Al - le -

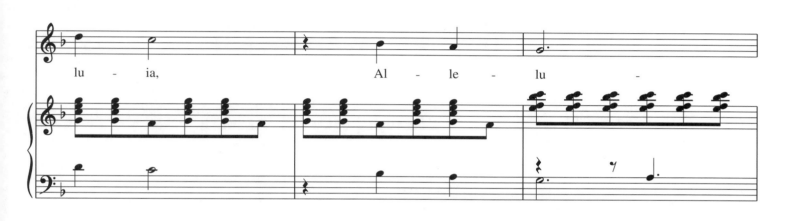

lu - ia, Al - le - lu -

ia! _____

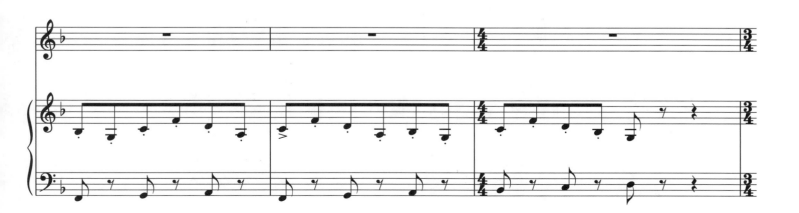

250

Thou flow-ing wa-ter, pure and clear, _____ Make

Thou flow-ing wa-ter, pure and clear, _____

mu-sic for thy Lord to hear, _____ Al-le-lu-ia, Al-le-

Make mu-sic for thy Lord to hear, _____ Al-le-

lu-ia! _____ Thou fire so mas-ter-ful and bright, That

lu-ia, Al-le-lu-ia! _____ Thou fire so mas-ter-ful and

giv - est man both warmth and light, _____ O __ praise Him, _____

bright, That giv - est man both warmth and light, O __

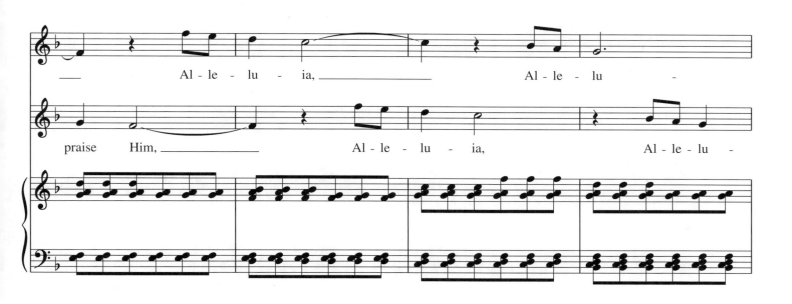

__ Al - le - lu - ia, _____ Al - le - lu -

praise Him, _____ Al - le - lu - ia, Al - le - lu -

ia! _____

ia! _____

accelerando poco a poco – – – – – – – – – – – – – – – – –

251

Fast

(repeat is optional)

(8va 2nd time - - - - - - - - -)

(repeat is optional)

rit.

8va - - - - -

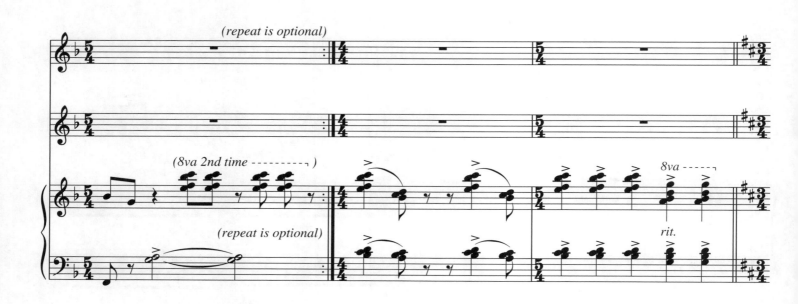

Maestoso

Praise God from whom all bles - sings

Let all things their cre - a - tor bless, And

mf warmly

8vb - - - - - - - - - - - - - - - - - - -

flow, Praise Him, all crea-tures here be - low;

wor-ship him in hum-ble - ness, O ___ praise Him, Al - le -

8vb

Praise Him a-bove, ye heav'n - ly host, _____ Praise

lu - ia! Praise, praise the Fa - ther, praise the

8vb

8vb

Fa - ther, Son and Ho - ly Ghost. _____

Son, And praise the Spi - rit, Three in One. _____

(8)

254

for Kimm

Come, Thou Fount of Every Blessing

Robert Robinson, 1758

American Folk Tune
First set by John Wyeth, 1813
arranged by Richard Walters

be! Let thy __ good-ness like a fet - ter Bind my wan-der-ing heart to __

Thee; Prone to __ wan - der, Lord I feel __ it, Prone to __ leave the God I ___

love; Here's my __ heart. O take and seal ___ it, Seal it for Thy courts a -

bove. ____

for Carol and Anne

How Can I Keep from Singing

American Folksong
Arranged by Richard Walters

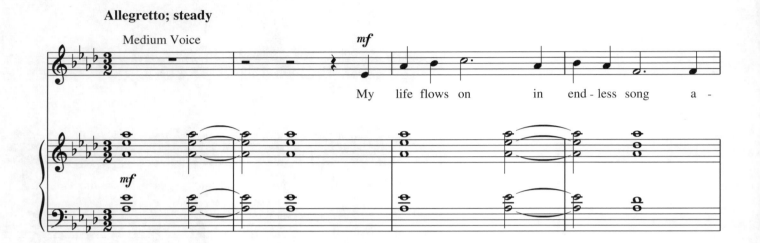

My life flows on in end-less song a-

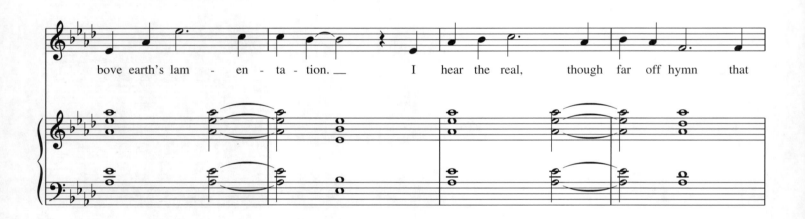

bove earth's lam - en - ta - tion. __ I hear the real, though far off hymn that

hails a new cre - a - tion. __ No storm can shake my in-most calm while

to that rock I'm cling-ing. __ Since love is lord of __ Heav'n and earth How

can I keep from sing - ing? __

High Voice

mf

When ty - rants trem - ble, sick with fear _____ And hear their death knells

Medium Voice *mf*

When ty - rants trem - ble, sick with fear And hear their death knells

like a sturdy hymn

for Russ and Rose Marie

How Firm A Foundation

John Rippon's *A Selection of Hymns,* 1787

Early American Melody
arranged by Richard Walters

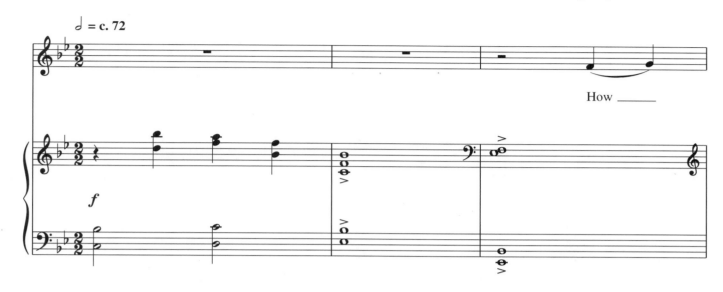

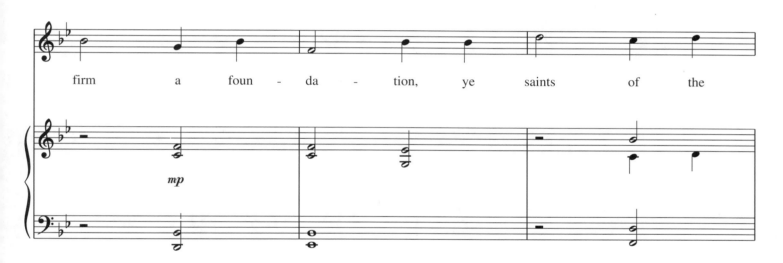

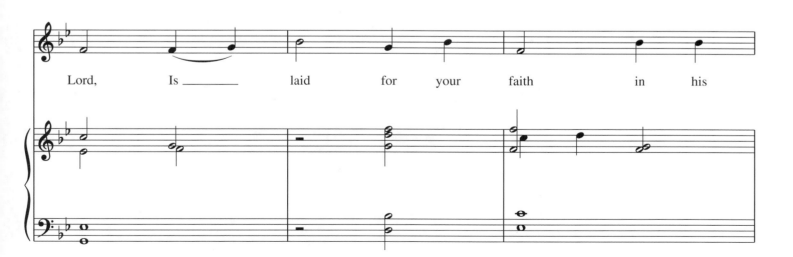

ex - cel - lent word! What more can he say than to

you he hath said, To _____ you who for ref - uge to

Je - sus have fled?

ni - po - tent hand.

mf

p cresc.

mf

decresc.

mp

p

When —

p

through the deep wa - ters I call thee to go, The —

riv - ers of woe shall not thee o - ver - flow; For

I will be near thee, thy trou - bles to bless, And ___

sanc - ti - fy to thee thy deep - est dis - tress.

for Robert

Let Us Break Bread Together

African–American Spiritual
arranged by Richard Walters

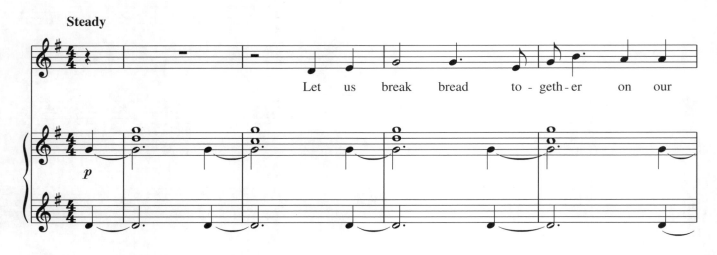

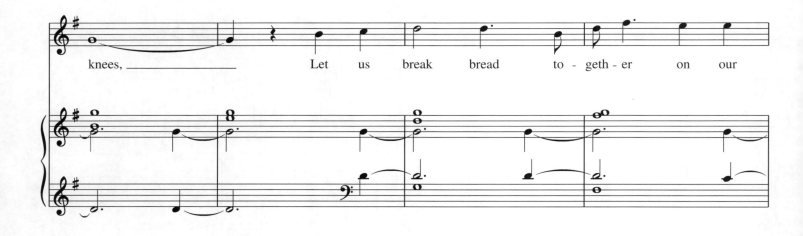

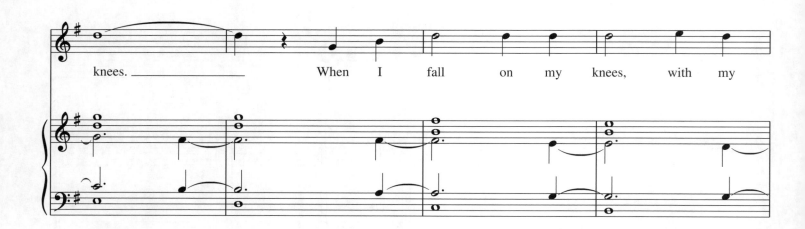

274

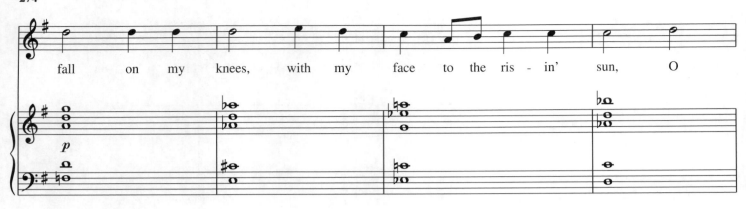

for Gayletha

Now Thank We All Our God

Martin Rinckart, c. 1636
translated by Catherine Winkworth, 1858

"Nun danket alle Gott"
melody by Johann Crüger, 1648
altered by Felix Mendelssohn, 1840
arranged by Richard Walters

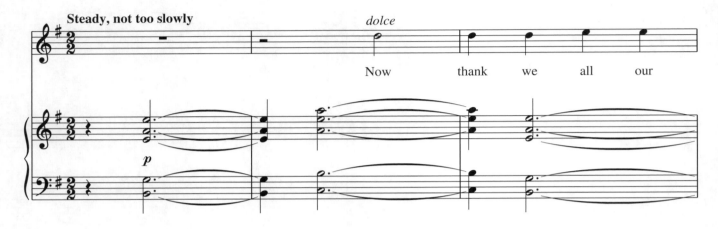

Now thank we all our

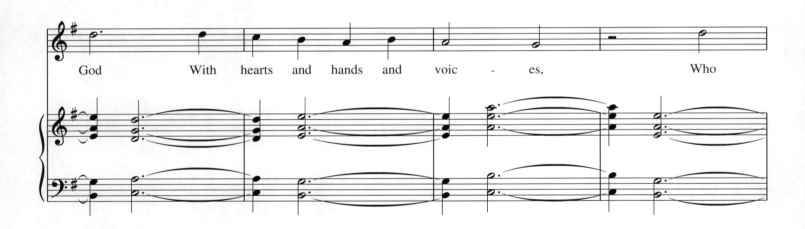

God   With hearts and hands and voic - es,   Who

won - d'rous things hath done,   In whom his world re - joic - es;

Who, from our moth-er's arms Hath blessed _ us on our

poco rit.

way With count-less gifts of love, And still is ours to-

day.

a tempo

O may this boun-teous God Through all our life be

near us, With ev - er joy - ful

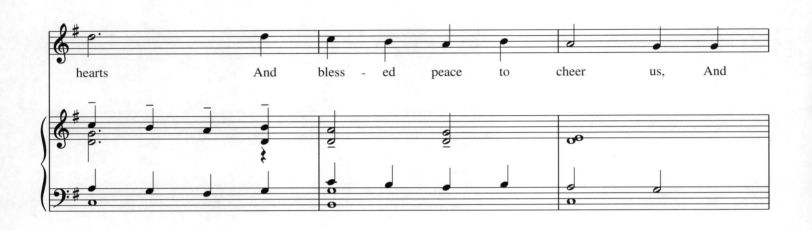

hearts And bless - ed peace to cheer us, And

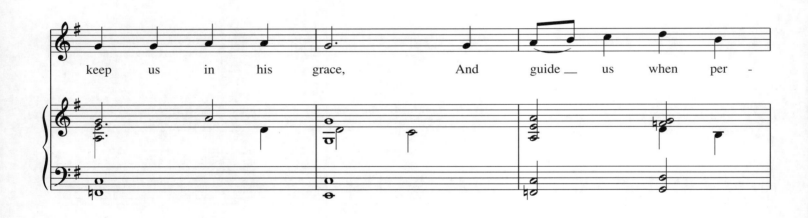

keep us in his grace, And guide __ us when per -

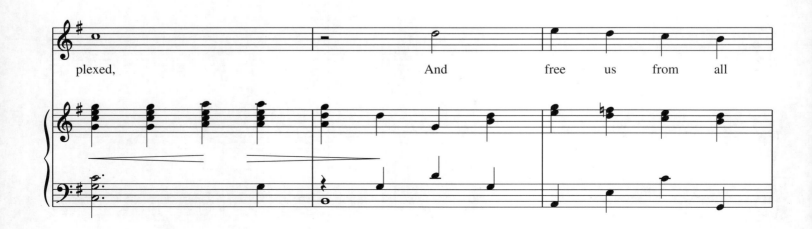

plexed, And free us from all

Son, and him who reigns with them in high-est heav-en,

The one e-ter-nal God, Whom

earth __ and heav'n a - dore For

thus it was, is now, And shall be __ ev - er more.

for Betsy and Harvey

O for a Thousand Tongues to Sing

Charles Wesley, 1739 (later altered)

Carl G. Gläser, 1784-1839
Mason's *Modern Psalmody,* 1839
arranged by Richard Walters

A firm moderato

O for a thou-sand tongues to sing My great Re-deem-er's

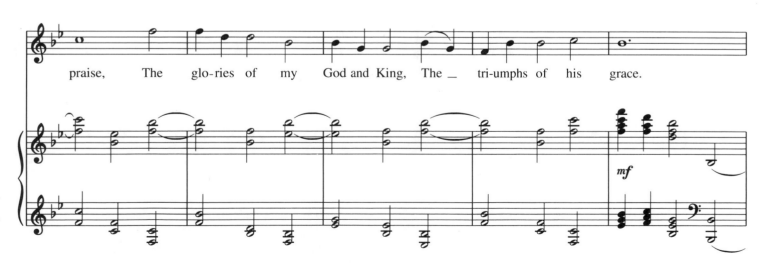

praise, The glo-ries of my God and King, The _ tri-umphs of his grace.

My gra-cious Mas - ter and my God, As - sist me to pro - claim, To spread thru all the earth a-broad The __ hon - ors of thy name.

A little slower

To God all glo - ry, praise and love Be now and ev - er

for Ida

Praise to the Lord,
the Almighty

after Psalm 103
Joachim Neander, 1680
translated by Catherine Winkworth and others

"Lobe den Herren"
Ernewerten Gesangbuch, Stralsund, 1665
arranged by Richard Walters

Brightly, in 1

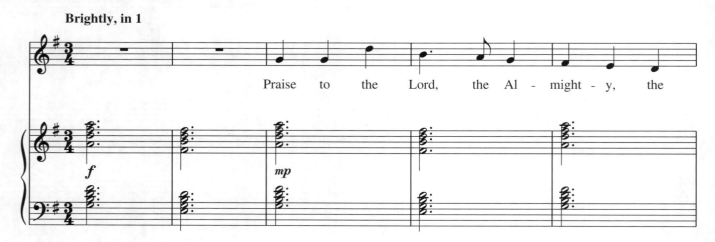

Praise to the Lord, the Al - might - y, the

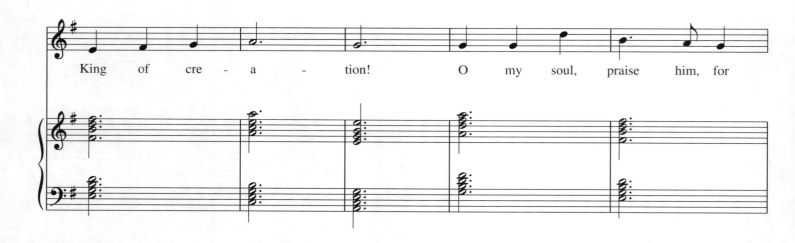

King of cre - a - tion! O my soul, praise him, for

he is thy health and sal - va - tion! Come, ye who

hear, Bro - thers and sis - ters draw near, Praise him in

glad ad - o - ra - tion!

Praise to the Lord, who o'er

all things so won - d'rous - ly reign - eth,

Shel - ters thee un - der his wings, yea, so gent - ly sus -

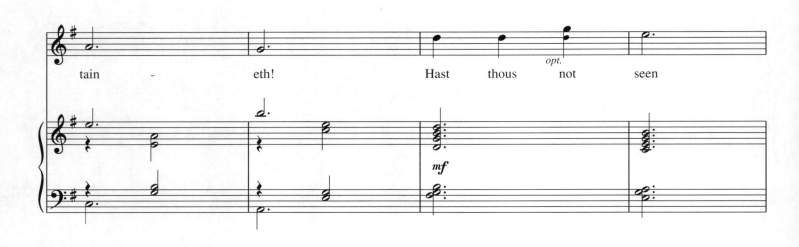

tain - eth! Hast thous not seen

All that is need - ful hath been Grant - ed in

what he or - dain - eth?

do, He who with love doth be - friend thee.

Praise to the Lord! O let all that is in me a - dore him!

All that hath life and breath, come now with

for Reed

This Is My Father's World

Maltbie D. Babcock, 1901

traditional English melody
first adapted by Franklin L. Sheppard, 1915
arranged by Richard Walters

With a light rock beat

legato, but rhythmic

This _ is my Fa - ther's

world, And _ to my lis - t'ning ears All na - ture sings, and _

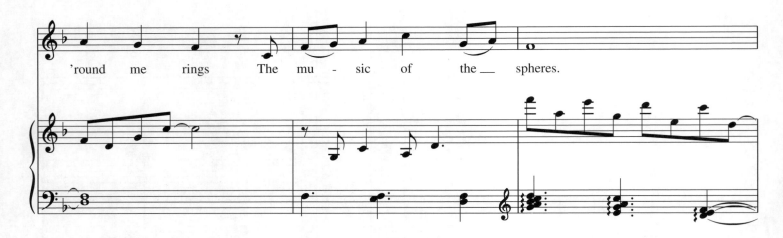

'round me rings The mu - sic of the _ spheres.

for Carol and Anne

We Are Climbing Jacob's Ladder

African-American Spiritual
Arranged by Richard Walters

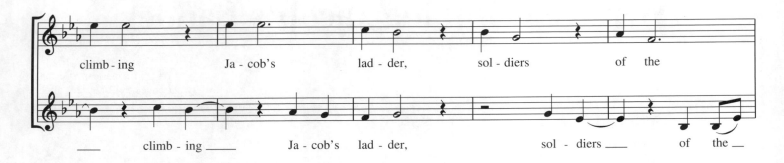

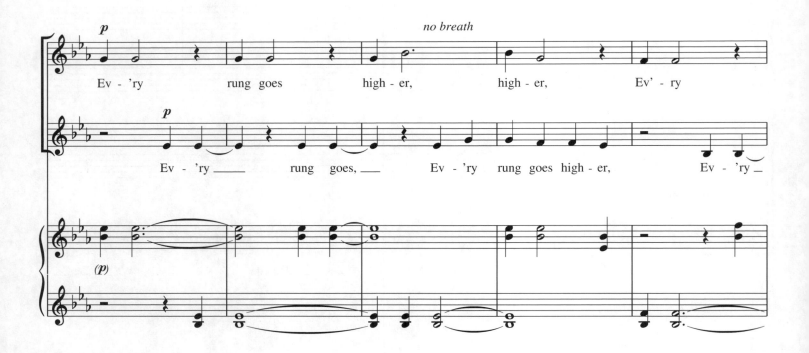

300

A Little Slower

We are climb - ing Ja - cob's lad - der, We are

We are climb - ing Ja - cob's gol - den lad - der We are

for Paul and Lou

Wondrous Love

American Folk Hymn
arranged by Richard Walters

lay a - side His crown for my soul, for my soul, He

soul, _____

O my

lay a - side His crown for my soul.

soul. _____

legato

mp

mp

High Voice:

What

won - drous love is this, O my soul, O my

Medium Voice:

What won - drous love is

soul, What won - drous love is this, O my

this, O my soul O my soul, What